INTO THE LONELY WOODS

Into the Lonely Woods

Published by Blue Angel Publishing®
80 Glen Tower Drive, Glen Waverley,
Victoria, Australia 3150
E-mail: info@blueangelonline.com
Website: www.blueangelonline.com

Editor: Natalie Stiles

Blue Angel is a registered trademark of
Blue Angel Gallery, Pty. Ltd.

ISBN: 978-1-922573-33-9

INTO THE LONELY WOODS

TRANSFORMING LONELINESS
INTO A QUEST OF THE SOUL

LUCY CAVENDISH
Artwork by DAN MAY

Blessed be, lonesome traveller.

YOU ARE A WISE ONE, setting

out now on the pilgrimage of the soul, travelling alone into the Lonely Woods for a time. And when you emerge and come back to yourself, to those you love and to those who love you, you will be transformed in enriching ways. This transformation will help you create beauty and magick wherever you go, even amidst your greatest challenges.

To use this book, simply turn to its wisdom whenever you feel discouraged or have need of inspiration and encouragement. Flick gently through the pages and stop when it feels right – this ancient art, known as bibliomancy, is the receiving of divine messages through a random reading of words in books. Do this, and you will find the words that speak to your soul at this time. Or, read through, page by page, until you feel comforted, protected, and perhaps even inspired to go on, filled with the knowledge that this lonely journey is a sacred quest.

Go with grace, be well, and be blessed.

BRIGHT SOUL, SECLUSION CAN BE AN OPPORTUNITY TO RECOVER YOUR TRUE HEART'S DESIRE.

How can you know what you truly want when all those about you tell me their ideas of who they think you are? When there is time alone, far from the same language or places and people, there in the stillness, your inner voice emerges. And this voice is filled with the love of your soul for yourself.

Whenever we are alone, our emotional response is complex
and multi-hued.

IF WE CHOOSE SECLUSION AFTER A TIME OF HIGH DEMAND, IT IS RELIEVING AND RESTORATIVE.

And we can find it healing after times of deep engagement and
connection to become only ourselves again for a while, to meet no
needs but our own — something so few of us experience regularly.
And yet, the soul requires this.

IT IS WISE FOR US ALL TO DEVELOP THE SENSE THAT TIME ALONE IS TIME VERY WELL SPENT.

This understanding will give us solace, offer great resilience, and create a sense of connection that no longer relies upon being with others. That does not mean we cannot have our kin or our family of people. It simply means that if we must walk alone for a time, we will find a way to do this and come to know who we are. Thus this time can be valuable, enriching, even joyous to experience.

SOME OF THE TROUBLES YOU CARRY ARE NOT YOURS — THEY DO NOT BELONG TO YOU.

And yet, you carry them. Share some of these concerns with a wise soul. They will help you know which of your troubles to keep, learn from and remember — and which burdens can be put aside, acknowledged as not yours to carry, and buried softly in the good earth to heal, change and become a part of the great all-that-is.

Love shall come in the simple tasks of life, and gratitude will flow from your heart. LIKE THE HUMMINGBIRD, YOU MAY FEEL SMALL, BUT YOU ARE CAPABLE OF THE MOST AMAZING FEATS. Your ability to change, adapt and recreate your own life now grows strong, and you come to respect your resilience, your playful nature, your natural optimism. All these abilities return, light as the hummingbird, sweet as the nectar of flowers.

You turned away from the voice of the world and listened instead to the wisdom of the growing world. Because of that, all is blossoming, rich, and verdant once again. You have made the wasteland a paradise. YOU HAVE SOWN THE SEEDS FROM WHICH BLESSINGS CAN NOW COME FORTH.

When we are alone, we learn how to not take our inspiration or sustenance from others. We do not drink from their wells. We do not feed from their cauldrons. We do not need anyone else's energy to generate our own. WITHIN YOU IS THE SPRING – DRINK FROM IT. Within you is the garden – water it. Find the source within you. Do not seek inspiration elsewhere — this is not the time for that connection. Now is the time to follow the path until you discover the grail of the self and become your own light.

YOU ARE SEEN, BEAUTIFUL SOUL.

Your isolation sometimes leads you to feel as though your existence will go unobserved. You are not invisible. You are seen and loved, even in these moments of absolute aloneness. The eyes of the spirit world watch over you more closely now than ever before. These beings, who dwell within all the elements, in every tree, in every breeze, within the deep and good earth, see you and wish to guide you. They are here to help you with what you need to know. Deepen your relationship with the true nature of this beautiful world. The owl knows your name and is calling you home.

From time to time, we must step outside our relationships with others to

CREATE A RELATIONSHIP WITH OURSELVES.

This is not loneliness. This is the true deep work of the becoming self, of the beckoning yearning to know the world on your own terms, even simply, through the senses. Become an island. Offer that alone time to your deepest self, and experience the world through the unfiltered truth of the self you are still becoming.

We bend, and we twist the self to please others, hiding most of who we are, showing only glimpses, for we fear rejection most of all. We never fully step out into the light to see who is drawn to the truth of who we are. Begin now by deepening the love of your own ways. Cease to speak words that appease others, yet offend your soul. Then offer that level of care and desire for love to yourself.

WHAT COULD YOU BECOME IF YOU ALREADY LOVED WHO YOU ARE?

SOME FRIENDSHIPS WITHSTAND DISTANCE, TIME APART, AND EVEN ENFORCED SEPARATIONS.

We set our course, and our paths may divert and part, but in time, they will converge again — joining as seamlessly as two rivers flowing into one, then parting again. Let the moments of true connection flow. When the time to be together comes again, those who truly love you will simply reach out their hand, open their arms, or even dance within the space that only your two energies combined can create.

Foolish, they say, to walk this strange path. Loneliness will become your only companion, they say, as you take those first steps on the lonesome road that leads to your true self. This is no adventure, no indulgence, no needless seeking. This is a pilgrimage of the soul, and the time you spend on the path may make you weary. There will be moments where your only companion is the voice inside your head. And that is the point.

WHEN YOU HEAR THAT VOICE CLEARLY, FOR ALMOST THE FIRST TIME, LISTEN.

And with each footstep, watch the words become more encouraging, loving, and filled with self-love.

YOUR INNER LIGHT WILL ILLUMINATE THE PATH

— the stony ground, the loose rocks, the thorns and ditches along the way. Keep your inner light burning bright, and trust the story unfolding beneath your feet. No one else can light your way. It is the light in your heart that will give you the greatest guidance when all about you falls into darkness. In time, the torch that you bear will become the light that inspires others to take up their torches and follow the radiance of their souls. You are the light that leads.

We can be different at night. It is liberating when the peace and silence, the stillness and strangeness, give us a chance to become something other than our daylight selves. NIGHT FEEDS THE SOULS WHO DARE TO DREAM WITH EYES WIDE OPEN, who take their visions and create lives of beauty and discomfort, who thrive amidst the wild, the bohemian, the nonconforming. This is what your soul craves — the song of the night, for the night self to arise, for the unshown self to be made visible, for the tattered wings you've tried too hard to hide to finally be seen by those with eyes of magick. The night will never be lonely again, for within it, you know you find yourself.

SOMETIMES the gulf between the old world and the world yet to come feels like a chasm. It doesn't feel possible to bridge that gap, to somehow make it to the other side. So, for a while, we slump and go into ourselves, into the denying and destructive old ways. And at this point, a sign will appear ... the scent of flowers, birdsong, the colours of dawn will give birth to hope in your heart ... and suddenly the gap will not seem so huge ... the waters you must cross will not seem so deep, nor will they feel dangerous ... and within a shorter while than you think possible, the old and the new will be bridged, and you will walk into the next life within this lifetime.

DEATH WALKS AMONGST US.

Within every breath and every step dwells the mortality so many deny. Do not fear this ending. Honour those who have left this life with ceremony, ritual, and respect. Learn to live with this truth, so that death is not a fearful enemy, but a gateway to another life. You have been so many forms already. But before you can transform again, we must pass through the great gateway, and allow our souls rest and freedom for a time. Only then can we choose wisely the next journey on the path of the soul.

We sculpt our lives until its shape is familiar, and we create patterns and stories, and rituals around these shapes, all of which make up the beautiful moments of our days. Our life is a whole world — and yet sometimes that world, through no decision we have made, comes to its ending, and all that once was will soon be the past. EVERY LIVING BEING IS IN FLUX. Take a moment to look upon what once was, to honour it, and say goodbye. Then stumble into the mysterious unknown, which holds what will become the beautiful future.

There will be times when the solitude feels blissful — the sensation of the air, the scent of the bud, the song of the bird, the wisdom of trees, the knowledge of the steady earth beneath your feet. When you are so full of the song of the world, you become one with the rhapsody of life. What once was a void has now become a world overflowing with delight and discovery. This ecstatic communion may never have been experienced had you not been in isolation for a time.

THERE ARE GIFTS HERE ON THE LONELY PATH. RECEIVE THEM, AND MAKE THEM YOURS.

Parts of us can become strangers. Yet, it is when we are alone that we can be most true and real. We live without artifice or the need to please or be pleased. Finally free, we can simply be. Do not make of this liberty a burden. Call back to yourself the wandering parts of your mind and soul that departed when they knew others could not understand them. COME TOGETHER, BE REUNITED WITHIN YOURSELF, AND FEEL THE MULTITUDE OF YOU.

You are a unique being, experiencing multiplicity through the oneness of your being. Let being alone for a time heal you, and **BRING YOU BACK FROM THE DARK PLACE THAT IS LONELINESS.** The comforting, healing qualities of solitude are yours — and these arrive spontaneously, unscheduled, without artifice. You truly love your own company.

The healer's touch may feel far from you, but if you allow the ancient ones to come to your aid, you will feel a tender hand upon your brow, offering you the energy of the Universe. ALLOW YOURSELF TO BE RESTORED BY THIS ANCIENT FORM OF BLESSING AND HEALING, even if human hands are far away right now. Imagine ... close those weary eyes ... know the ancient ones are with you and let them reweave the fibres of light that make you into the being of radiance you so truly are.

Being alone for a time can mean we start to understand what our stories have become far more deeply — and we begin to know how our stories need to change. The tale of your life now becomes more and more clearly written by your own self, without all the suggestions and interruptions— even those that are well-meant—of others. Let the truth become clearer, and clearer, until it is in front of you.

THIS TRUTH IS YOUR STORY. AND IT IS YOURS TO WRITE.

There will be times when being alone can make us feel so very small and full of doubt. Questions mutter into the ache of our being: Do I matter? Do others care? Why do I feel so lost? At first, the vastness of the silence that greets these questions may seem to confirm our insignificance. But in time, you will feel a belonging, as if you fit within the greater design of the world. YOU ARE SIGNIFICANT, FOR YOU ARE A CHILD OF THIS PLANET, AND YOU BELONG HERE.

It seems lonelier at night, somehow. In darkness, we become strange as moonlight. Yet, by entering the void of night, you bring your magickal self to life. The dawn will come. BUT LET THE NIGHT'S PECULIAR LIGHT ILLUMINATE THE WILD WORLD THAT RESIDES WITHIN YOU. When you do this, what was once unseen will reveal itself and share the road with you, enriching every day with its divinity.

SO OFTEN, WE ARE DISTRACTED — we plough

through the day, too busy to see or hear, to feel and to think. And the deep

soul starves within us. The key to moving into a more soulful and rich

connection with yourself and the world lies in these more lonesome times.

You will have moments of realisation that are the key to your entire life

taking a different shape in the days to come — and this is a great blessing,

born from the quiet, the stillness, the space around and within us in

isolation.

THE WELL is the memory, the reservoir of the ancestors, the emotional world where those parts of your self and soul live, patiently awaiting you. Gaze down the well. Conjure up the lost selves. Up they rise, to join you again. Give them space to share their wise stories with you. For nothing that belongs to you can ever be lost. It is only that, for a time, you forgot the blessings of all that you are.

Even though the time has passed for your tales to intertwine,

the loosening of the bonds of love need not be bitter.

For now, you must take your leave.

YOU WILL NOT BE LOST WHEN YOU FOLLOW THE DARKENING PATH INTO THE UNKNOWN.

Be content with the light you carry within

and the light you have lit within others.

These will be the guides on the mysterious path before you.

ENDINGS OPEN THE SPACE FOR BEGINNINGS. Because you

let go, a beginning is on its way, made more magickal and beautiful because

you made space for it. The self that held on so tight had no space to receive.

Now you know that when you let go, a sacred space is made, and into that

space will walk the wonder.

THERE IS ONE WHO HAS ALWAYS WATCHED OVER YOU, compassionate and sage,

but never interfering with your free will. To know you have this guardian is to understand that, while although there is loneliness, you are never alone. Your Watcher is linked to the path of your soul, from your first breath to your last, and they will be with you in the great in-between of your lifetimes. The one who watches over you knows the sacred quest of your soul, and when it sees that you have lost your way, they will come to you in blessed ways to remind you to go on. Your soul knows the way.

SOON will come a reunion, a beautiful homecoming — a time of enrichment, and contentment. The solitude you have experienced means you have more to share, more than ever before. Because of your transformation, these soul companions can see you, understand you, accept you, love you, reach for you in the morning and kiss you as you fall asleep. The time of solitude shaped your soul. And the shape it took has become beautiful indeed.

Your unfelt emotions, the mysteries of the psyche, the flowing nature of who you are fearful to be — all these mysteries can now be explored.

SINK INTO THE SUBCONSCIOUS, AND KNOW IT IS SAFE FOR YOU TO BE WITHIN THIS WATERY PLACE.

Feel the gift of the silence, the calm, the weightlessness, and the depth of this world. You are a part of this, just as you are a part of the air. The beauty of water will open your eyes to the beauty of the emotions within you.

Take comfort in knowing that there are others like you, and in time, your paths may meet. Others like you are experiencing an awakening. The truth you are awakening to is the changing nature of your being, the way we have life, within life, within life. It seems as if you are the only one experiencing such a profound rebirth, and this can lead you to feel bleak, believing that there is no one else who has experienced quite what you have. This is true. Your experience is unique and profound. But other souls are gently seeing the possibilities of their own freedom. They walk their own path, shunning the loud voices of the human world that shout their empty words into numb ears and blank minds. THERE ARE OTHERS LIKE YOU. You are not alone in this rebirthing of the inner and outer worlds.

TRUE COMMUNION comes in

the moments where two, who once felt like strangers, connect over the simple delight of the warmth that springs up between them. Our souls, for all that they grow in solitude, crave those moments of connection. And here you have this moment. This kinship is created through what is shared but unspoken, what is understood without explanation, what is seen without being revealed. The tender part of each of you has found a safe place, each within the other. Nurture this gently and with respect. In time, let us see what will be woven between your two souls. For now, rest in the bliss of this communion.

When you find others who have found kinship and contentment, learn of their rites. Which could you share? Would you then make time for play, delight, and celebration in your life? This is a time for the new, for the unlearned, for the joyous discovery of what could be and what will come. Anticipate this with all the sweetness you can muster,

and LEARN FROM THOSE WHO HAVE FOUND A WAY TO LIVE TOGETHER WELL.

A SWEET, SMALL BLESSING

will open your energy to receive even more joy. Destiny wishes you to be content, to feel loved, and to see the wonder in every small thing. Look about you — for right there, in the smallest of places, are the blessings you have been yearning for. Open your new eyes to the world — and what once went unseen and unappreciated can be truly known for the very first time.

IT IS TIME TO REST A WHILE, BEAUTIFUL SOUL.

This rest is when some of your most sacred work is done: in dreams, in the cocoon, you create as you separate from the exterior and enter deeply into the divine universe that dwells within you. It is time to restore and regenerate, to recreate and reweave the inner world — that sanctuary, the memory palace and beautiful grove where all true healing takes place. While the world of Nature is a-resting, you too must return to the deep for this phase of the cycle of life. Slumber and dream, so you can emerge renewed.

There will again come a time of shared experiences, their pleasures amplified because they are mutual. This is the true joy of companionship and friendship — that sense that the world is seen and experienced and even understood for a small moment by two or more people.

ALL IS SWEETER BECAUSE THE DEEP LONGING TO SHARE WITH ANOTHER IS FINALLY FULFILLED.

When the reunion comes, it will be blessed, pure, and so full of joy that you will not regret the time that took you from each other. The time you have will be so full of love and kindness, of recognition and support, it will transform all the days of your life. Your life will become a tapestry woven of love. **YOU ARE HELD, SUPPORTED, SEEN, AND HEARD.** This reunion, this union of two renewed souls, is blessed.

Dear friend, the world now opens up to you. Into the great depths, you plunged, your soul a-tattered, your heart in pieces, your hands closed and tight. And now you have found your way in the endless beneath. Your hands have a gentle touch, and draw to you the shyest of creatures. They know you are, above all, an ally, kin, and friend to the shyest of beings with their rare nature. You have found a home, and you are creating your destiny, which is clear, brighter, higher, and more filled with joy and blessings than you could ever have imagined. DIVE DOWN INTO THE HIDDEN PLACES, BRIGHT SOUL, and ready your heart for waves of joy.

LUCY CAVENDISH is a Witch

and spiritual author. She exhibited strong extra-sensory abilities as a child. With no answers from school or mainstream religion, Lucy set out on a personal quest to understand and develop her magickal gifts.

Lucy grew up in Sydney, Australia, and has lived in Paris, London, and the United States. Today she is an exciting, enchanting voice in the field of inspiration, noted for her breadth and depth of knowledge on sacred rites and sites, magickal history, witchcraft, folklore, alternative spiritual practices, and intuitive traditions.

Lucy shares her knowledge and gifts to inspire intuitive people to break through their conditioning, open up to their potential, discover their personal power, and dare to live brave, bright, authentic lives. Lucy's teachings are about spirited self-development, and her intuitive training embraces both shadows and light. She is remarkable for her vision, compassion, wisdom, humour and insight.

Lucy lectures and teaches around the world. Her books and oracle decks are available in many languages, and she's a popular guest on television programs such as *Studio Ten*, *The Project* and *The Morning Show*. She began a podcast in 2019 called *The Witchcast*, which reaches thousands of seekers every week. Her work has struck a chord with contemporary seekers ready to create lives of courage, spiritual adventure, and enriching magick. When she's not writing or speaking or recording, you'll find Lucy surfing in the ocean, wandering deep within a faery forest, or dancing with the spirits in an ancient stone circle.

You can find out more about Lucy by visiting her website:
www.lucycavendish.com.au

DAN MAY is a modern narrative

painter. A native of Rochester, NY, Dan attended Syracuse University where he achieved a BFA and immediately began to pursue his artistic interests. May weaves a rich texture of the surreal and mysterious into his highly original flowing style. His detail-intensive works have become widely recognised for their dreamlike ability to transcend the natural states of space and time. His paintings have been exhibited in galleries and museums throughout the world, including the 2013 *Suggestivism* show at the Acquario Romano in Rome. Dan lives and works in Northern Michigan with his wife, Kendal and their three children.

www.danmay.net

For more information on this or any
Blue Angel Publishing release,
visit our website:

www.blueangelonline.com